American Thread Co.

STAR STOLE BOOK No. 133

10 CENTS

Stoles

KNITTED • CROCHETED
HAIRPIN LACE

Stoles

As beautiful as notes in a new song ... as soft as sweet music when made with "Dawn" Wools, Nylon or Orlons.

We have collected a beautiful group for you to knit, crochet, or make with hairpin lace. We hope you'll like them.

The American Thread Company 260 W. BROADWAY,
NEW YORK 13, N. Y.

---

* (Asterisk)—This sign indicates that the instructions immediately following are to be repeated the given number of times plus the original.

** Are used in the same way.

Adagio—The Collar Stole—Illustrated On Cover

21 inches x 68 inches

Materials Required:

AMERICAN THREAD COMPANY

"DAWN" KNITTING WORSTED
22 ounces Dk. Violet or color of your choice
1 pr. knitting needles No. 7

Gauge: 9 sts = 1½ inches 10 rows = 1½ inches

Cast on 123 stitches (sts), work in pattern as follows:

1st Row: Knit (K) 3, * Purl (P) 3, K 3, repeat from * across row.

2nd Row: K 3, K 3 together (tog), * P 3, K 3 tog, repeat from * across row ending with K 3.

3rd Row: * K 3, yarn over (y o), slip (sl) the next st as if to P, repeat from * across row ending with K 3.

4th Row: K 3, * insert needle through next st and y o and K 1, y o, K 1 in same st, sl both y o and st off needle (3 sts made), P 3, repeat from * across row, ending last repeat with K 3.

5th Row: K 3, * P 3, K 3, repeat from * across row.

6th Row: K 6, P 3, * K 3, P 3, repeat from * across row ending with K 6.

7th Row: K 3, P 3, * K 3 tog, P 3, repeat from * across row, ending with K 3.

8th Row: K 6, * y o, sl 1, K 3, repeat from * across row ending last repeat with K 6.

9th Row: K 3, P 3, * insert needle through next st and y o, K 1, y o, K 1 in same st, drop both y o and st off needle, P 3, repeat from * across row ending with K 3.

10th Row: Same as 6th row.

11th Row: Same as 5th row.

Repeat from 2nd through 11th row until stole measures 66 inches from beginning ending with 5th row of pattern, bind off in pattern. Block to measurement.

Collar: Cast on 141 sts, K 3, * P 3, K 3, repeat from * across row. Repeat from 2nd through 11th row same as on stole 5 times.

Next 5 Rows: K across each row. Bind off. This is outside edge of collar. Fold collar in half and place a pin at inside edge. Fold stole in half and place a pin. Sew collar to stole matching pins.

Allegro

20 inches x 66 inches without fringe

Materials Required:

AMERICAN THREAD COMPANY

"DAWN" BULKY YARN
16 ounces White or color of your choice
1 pr. wooden knitting needles No. 11
Plastic crochet hook size H

Gauge: Each pattern measures 3¾ inches in width

1st Section: Cast on 63 stitches (sts) and work in pattern as follows:

1st Row: Knit (K) 1, K 2 together (tog), * K 9, slip (sl) 1, K 2 tog, pass slip stitch over K st (p.s.s.o.), repeat from * 3 times, K 9, K 2 tog, K 1.

2nd Row: K 1, Purl (P) across row to within last st, K 1.

3rd Row: K 1, K 2 tog, * K 7, sl 1, K 2 tog, p.s.s.o., repeat from * 3 times, K 7, K 2 tog, K 1.

4th Row: Repeat 2nd row.

5th Row: K 1, K 2 tog, * yarn over (y o), K 1, repeat from * 4 times, y o, sl 1, K 2 tog, p.s.s.o., repeat from 1st * 3 times, (y o, K 1) 5 times, y o, K 2 tog, K 1.

6th Row: K across row, work should now measure 1½ inches when blocked. Repeat these 6 rows 23 more times. Place all these sts on a strand of yarn, cut yarn. Make another section in same manner but ending with

5th row of pattern, leave on needle, cut yarn. Place right side of both sections together and with free needle, * sl 1 st from 1st section, sl 1 st from 2nd section, repeat from * until all sts are on 1 needle. Bind off as follows: attach yarn at beginning of row, K 2 sts tog, K the next 2 sts tog, * pass the 1st st over the 2nd st, K the next 2 sts tog again having 2 sts on needle, repeat from * until one st remains. Cut yarn and draw through remaining loop.

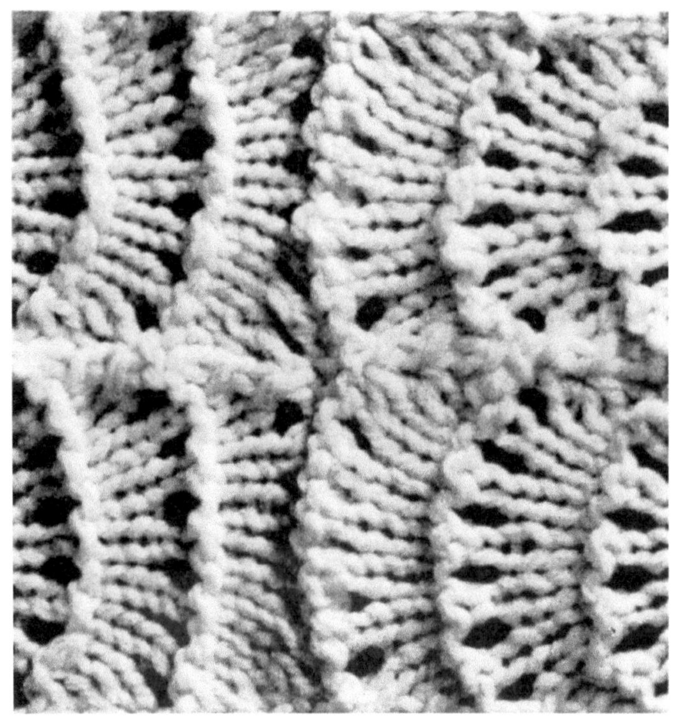

Edge: With wrong side of work toward you attach yarn at lower edge and work loosely a row of sl sts across side, cut yarn. Finish other long side in same manner.

Fringe: Wind yarn over an 8 inch cardboard, cut one end. Using 1 strand, double in half and knot through each st across short end.

Next Row: * Take 1 strand of yarn of 1 fringe and 1 strand from next fringe, knot tog about ½ inch from preceding row of knots, repeat from * across row. Repeat last row twice. Trim fringe evenly. Finish other end in same manner.

Harmony

20 inches x 66 inches without fringe

Materials Required:

AMERICAN THREAD COMPANY

"DAWN" KNEELING WORSTED
20 ounces White or color of your choice
1 pr. knitting needles No. 10

Gauge: 9 garter sts = 2 inches

Cast on 84 stitches (sts) and work in pattern as follows:

1st, 2nd, 3rd and 4th Rows: Knit (K) across each row.

5th Row: * Insert needle in st, yarn over (y o) needle 3 times, pull through st, slip (sl) st off needle, repeat from * across row.

6th Row: * Sl 6 sts on right hand needle dropping the y o's, sl them back on left hand needle by inserting needle in 3rd, 2nd and 1st st in front of work passing them over the last 3 sts, then sl the last 3 sts on left hand needle (thus twisting sts), K 6 sts picking up back loop of each st, repeat from * across row.

Repeat these 6 rows for pattern until stole measures 66 inches from beginning ending with the 4th row of pattern, bind off.

Fringe: Wind yarn over a 14 inch cardboard, cut one end. Using 3 strands, double in half and knot fringe in every other st across each end.

* Take half of one group of fringe and half of next group of fringe, knot together ¾ inch from 1st row of knots, repeat from * across row, then repeat from 1st * for another row of knots. Trim fringe evenly. Finish other end in same manner.

Symphony

Materials Required:

AMERICAN THREAD COMPANY

"DAWN" BULKY YARN
12 ounces Black
¾ yd. White Tubular Jersey or color of your choice

Turn inward a small hem on one cut edge of material and baste together. Slip stitch edges together. Work opposite side in same manner.

Fringe: Cut yarn into 46 inch lengths. With a large needle make a hole in one corner of material, take 3 strands of yarn, double in half, loop through hole, draw ends through loop tightly. * Make another hole about ½ inch from previous hole, take 3 strands of yarn, double in half, loop through hole, draw ends through loop tightly, repeat from * 3 times. * Make another hole about 1¼ inches from previous hole, make a fringe in hole in same manner, repeat from * 19 times (last fringe should be about 2 inches from next corner). Work 4 more fringes in same manner ½ inch apart having last fringe in corner. Repeat from 1st * all around ending to correspond.

2nd Row: Take half of one group of fringe and half of next group of fringe and knot together about 1 inch from previous row of knots. Repeat 2nd row 5 times. Trim fringe evenly.

Crescendo

19 INCHES x 66 INCHES WITHOUT FRINGE

Materials Required:

AMERICAN THREAD COMPANY

"DAWN" KNITTING WORSTED
20-ounces Violet or color of your choice
1 pair knitting needles No. 13
1 double pointed needle

Gauge: 1 cable crossing = 1¼ inches

Cast on 100 stitches (sts).

1st Row: Knit (K) across row.

2nd Row: K 2, Purl (P) to within 2 sts, K 2.

3rd Row: K 2, * slip (sl) 3 sts on a double pointed needle and hold in back of work, K 3, K 3 sts from double pointed needle, repeat from * across row to within 2 sts, K 2.

4th Row: Same as 2nd row.

5th Row: K across row.

6th Row: Same as 2nd row.

7th Row: K 5, * sl 3 sts on a double pointed needle and hold in front of work, K 3, K 3 sts from double pointed needle, repeat from * to within 5 sts, K 5.

8th Row: Same as 2nd row.

Repeat these 8 rows until stole measures 66 inches, then K 1 row, P 1 row. Bind off loosely.

FRINGE: Wind yarn over an 8 inch cardboard, cut one end. Using 6 strands, double in half and loop through each cable crossing on short sides.

Contralto

64 inches in length

Materials Required:

AMERICAN THREAD COMPANY

"DAWN" BULKY YARN
20 ounces Light Blue or color of your choice
1 pr. wooden knitting needles No. 11
1 double pointed needle
Aluminum crochet hook size I

Gauge: 7 garter sts = 2 inches5 garter st rows = 1 inch

Cast on 30 stitches (sts) and work in garter st [Knit (K) each row] for 11 inches.

Next Row: Increase 5 sts evenly spaced. Work in pattern as follows:

1st Row: K 5, * slip (sl) 1, K 1, pass slip st over K st (p.s.s.o.), yarn over (y o), K 1, y o, K 2 together (tog), K 5, repeat from * across row.

2nd Row: K 5, * Purl (P) 5, K 5, repeat from * across row. Repeat 1st and 2nd rows twice.

7th Row: K 5, * sl the next 3 sts on a double pointed needle and hold in back of work, K the next 2 sts, replace the last st on double pointed needle onto the left hand needle and K this st, K the 2 remaining sts from opposite end of double pointed needle, K 5, repeat from * across row.

8th Row: Same as 2nd row. Repeat the last 8 rows once.

17th Row: Increase (inc) in 1st st, K 4, * sl 1, K 1, p.s.s.o., y o, K 1, y o, K 2 tog, K 5, repeat from * across row.

18th Row: Same as 2nd row but end with P 1.

19th Row: Increase in 1st st, then work same as 1st row.

20th Row: Same as 2nd row but end with P 1, inc in last st.

21st Row: Inc in 1st st, K 2, then work the remainder of row same as 1st row.

22nd Row: Same as 2nd row but end with P 3, inc in next st.

23rd Row: Slip 1st 3 sts on a double pointed needle and hold in back of work, K the next 2 sts, replace the last st on double pointed needle onto left hand needle and K this st, K the 2 remaining sts from opposite end of double pointed needle, K 5, * sl the next 3 sts on double pointed needle and hold in back of work, K the next 2 sts, replace the last st on double pointed needle onto left hand needle and K this st, K the 2 remaining sts from opposite end of double pointed needle, K 5, repeat from * across row.

24th Row: Same as 2nd row but end with P 5.

25th Row: Inc in 1st st, K 1, y o, K 1, y o, K 2 tog, then work same as 1st row.

26th Row: * K 5, P 5, repeat from * across row ending with K 2.

27th Row: Inc in 1st st, K 1, * sl 1, K 1, p.s.s.o., y o, K 1, y o, K 2 tog, K 5, repeat from * across row.

28th Row: * K 5, P 5, repeat from * across row ending with K 2, inc in next st.

29th Row: Inc in 1st st, K 3, * sl 1, K 1, p.s.s.o., y o, K 1, y o, K 2 tog, K 5, repeat from * across row.

30th Row: Same as 2nd row.

31st Row: Same as 7th row.

32nd Row: Same as 2nd row.

Repeat from the 17th through the 32nd row 3 times.

Repeat from the 17th through the 24th row once.

Next Row: K 2, y o, K 1, y o, K 2 tog, then work same as 1st row.

Next Row: * K 5, P 5, repeat from * across row ending with K 1.

Next Row: K 1, * sl 1, K 1, p.s.s.o., y o, K 1, y o, K 2 tog, K 5, repeat from * across row.

Next Row: * K 5, P 5, repeat from * across row ending with K 1.

Next Row: K 1, * sl 1, K 1, p.s.s.o., y o, K 1, y o, K 2 tog, K 5, repeat from * across row.

Next Row: * K 5, P 5, repeat from * across row ending with K 1.

Next Row: K 1, * sl next 3 sts on a double pointed needle and hold in back of work, K 2, replace the last st on double pointed needle onto left hand needle and K this st, K the 2 remaining sts from opposite end of double pointed needle, K 5, repeat from * across row.

Next Row: * K 5, P 5, repeat from * across row ending with K 1.

Next Row: K 1, * sl 1, K 1, p.s.s.o., y o, K 1, y o, K 2 tog, K 5, repeat from * across row. Repeat last 8 rows 12 times.

Next Row: * K 5, P 5, repeat from * across row ending with K 1.

Next Row: K 2 tog (y o, K 2 tog) twice, K 5, * sl 1, K 1, p.s.s.o., y o, K 1, y o, K 2 tog, K 5, repeat from * across row.

Next Row: * K 5, P 5, repeat from * across row.

Next Row: (K 2 tog) 3 times, K 4, * sl 1, K 1, p.s.s.o., y o, K 1, y o, K 2 tog, K 5, repeat from * across row.

Next Row: * K 5, P 5, repeat from * across row ending last repeat with P 2.

Next Row: K 7, * cable twist over next 5 sts, K 5, repeat from * across row.

Next Row: K 5, * P 5, K 5, repeat from * across row ending with P 2 tog.

Next Row: K 2 tog, K 4, * sl 1, K 1, p.s.s.o., y o, K 1, y o, K 2 tog, K 5, repeat from * across row.

Next Row: K 5, * P 5, K 5, repeat from * across row.

Next Row: K 2 tog, K 3, * sl 1, K 1, p.s.s.o., y o, K 1, y o, K 2 tog, K 5, repeat from * across row.

Next Row: * K 5, P 5, repeat from * across row ending with K 4.

Next Row: K 2 tog, K 2, * sl 1, K 1, p.s.s.o., y o, K 1, y o, K 2 tog, K 5, repeat from * across row.

Next Row: * K 5, P 5, repeat from * across row ending with K 3.

Next Row: K 2 tog, K 1, * cable twist over next 5 sts, K 5, repeat from * across row.

Next Row: * K 5, P 5, repeat from * across row ending with K 2.

Next Row: K 2 tog, * sl 1, K 1, p.s.s.o., y o, K 1, y o, K 2 tog, K 5, repeat from * across row. Repeat the last 16 rows 3 times.

Next Row: * K 5, P 5, repeat from * across row ending with K 1.

Next Row: K 2 tog (y o, K 2 tog) twice, K 5, * sl 1, K 1, p.s.s.o., y o, K 1, y o, K 2 tog, K 5, repeat from * across row.

Next Row: * K 5, P 5, repeat from * across row.

Next Row: (K 2 tog) 3 times, K 4, * sl 1, K 1, p.s.s.o., y o, K 1, y o, K 2 tog, K 5, repeat from * across row.

Next Row: * K 5, P 5, repeat from * across row ending last repeat with P 2.

Next Row: K 7, * cable twist over next 5 sts, K 5, repeat from * across row.

Next Row: K 5, * P 5, K 5, repeat from * across row ending with P 2 tog.

Next Row: K 2 tog, K 4, * sl 1, K 1, p.s.s.o., y o, K 1, y o, K 2 tog, K 5, repeat from * across row.

Next Row: Same as 2nd row.

Next Row: Same as 1st row.

Next Row: Same as 2nd row.

Next Row: Same as 1st row.

Next Row: Same as 2nd row.

Next Row: Same as 7th row.

Next Row: Same as 2nd row.

Next Row: Same as 1st row. Repeat the last 8 rows once. Repeat the 2nd row and 1st row once.

Next Row: K across row decreasing 5 sts evenly spaced. Work even in garter st until garter st section measures 11 inches ending on right side, bind off.

Fold each garter st section in half on wrong side. Sew side edges together. Turn inside out and sew top edge of pockets about 1 inch in from each side. With right side of work toward you and working along curved edge, attach yarn at top of pocket and work a row of single crochet (sc) along curved edge to top of other pocket.

Sonata

22 inches x 68 inches without fringe

Materials Required:

AMERICAN THREAD COMPANY

"DAWN" or "CLOVERLEAF"
NYLON or
NYLON POMPADOUR or
"DAWN" MEDIUM WEIGHT
POMPADOUR or
"DAWN" BABY YARN
10 ounces BABY LAVENDER or
ORCHID or color of your choice
1 pr. plastic knitting needles No. 6

Gauge: 6 garters sts = 1 inch

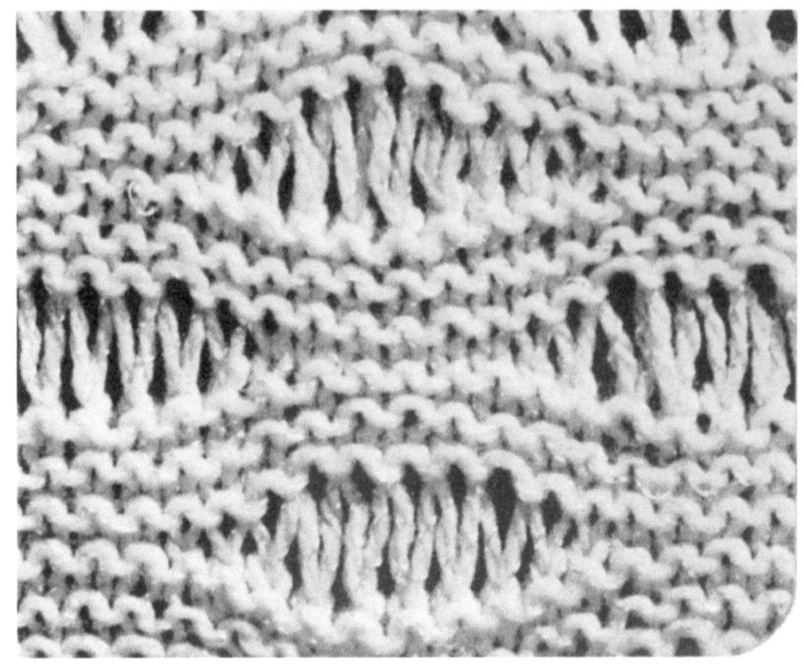

Cast on 133 stitches (sts) and work in garter st [knit (K) each row] for 1¼ inches, then work in pattern as follows:

1st Row: K 7, ** yarn over (y o), K 1, * y o twice, K 1, repeat from * 4 times, y o, K 8, repeat from ** across row.

2nd Row: ** K 8, drop y o from previous row off needle (all y o's are dropped without working them), K 1, * drop the next 2 y o's off needle, K 1, repeat from * 4 times, drop the next y o off needle, repeat from ** across row ending with K 7.

Next 4 Rows: K across each row.

7th Row: K 14, ** y o, K 1, * y o twice, K 1, repeat from * 4 times, y o, K 8, repeat from ** across row ending last repeat with K 15.

8th Row: K 15, ** drop y o off needle, K 1, * drop the next 2 y o's off needle, K 1, repeat from * 4 times, drop the next y o off needle, K 8, repeat from ** across row ending last repeat with K 14.

9th through 13th Rows: K across each row.

Repeat last 13 rows 33 times.

Repeat 1st and 2nd rows once. Work even in garter st for 1¼ inches, bind off. Block to measurements.

Fringe: Wind yarn over a 10 inch cardboard, cut one end.

Using 5 strands, double in half and knot through center st of last 2 rows at lower edge every 5th st across end.

* Take half of one group of fringe and half of next group of fringe, knot together ½ inch from 1st row of knots, epeat from * across row. Repeat last row of knots twice, trim evenly. Finish opposite end to correspond.

Waltz

Materials Required:

AMERICAN THREAD COMPANY

"DAWN" BULKY YARN
7 ounces Buttercup for 15 inch length cape
8 ounces Buttercup for 19 inch length cape and
The Famous "PURITAN" STAR SPANGLED MERCERIZED CROCHET COTTON, Article 40
2 balls Gold Spangle or colors of your choice
1—4 inch hairpin lace staple
1—3 inch hairpin lace staple
1—2 inch hairpin lace staple
Plastic crochet hook size F
Steel crochet hook No. 7
2 hooks and eyes

Hairpin Lace: Make a loop at end of yarn and place left prong of staple in loop just made, wind yarn around right prong of hairpin staple, insert plastic crochet hook in loop, yarn over hook and draw loop through keeping work at center of staple, * drop loop from hook, turn staple ½ turn to the left, pick up the dropped loop at center, yarn over and pull through loop, insert hook through top part of loop on left hand prong, yarn over and pull through (2 loops on hook), yarn over and pull through both loops completing the single crochet (sc), repeat from * for desired length.

All strips are worked with Buttercup and size F hook.

For 15 inch length cape work 1st 5 strips.

For 19 inch length cape work 6 strips.

1st Strip: With 2 inch staple work a length of hairpin lace having 89 loops on each side of staple.

2nd Strip: With 2 inch staple work a length having 133 loops on each side of staple.

3rd Strip: With 3 inch staple work a length having 155 loops on each side of staple.

4th Strip: With 3 inch staple work a length having 177 loops on each side of staple.

5th Strip: With 4 inch staple work a length having 199 loops on each side of staple.

6th Strip: With 4 inch staple work a length having 221 loops on each side of staple.

Note: When working strips, twists are taken out of all groups of loops and twist is left in all single loops. This will not be referred to again.

Short Cape: With steel crochet hook attach Gold Spangle in 1st loop of the 2 inch hairpin lace strip of 89 loops, sc in same space, 1 sc in each of the next 2 loops, * ch 1, 1 sc in each of the next 3 loops, repeat from * across row ending last repeat with 1 sc in each of the next 2 loops, cut thread.

Working on opposite side of same strip attach Gold Spangle in 1st hairpin lace loop, * ch 5, sc in next loop, repeat from * across row, cut thread.

2nd Strip: With Gold Spangle and 2 inch hairpin lace strip of 133 loops, attach thread in 1st loop, ch 2, sc in last loop worked of 1st strip, ch 2, sc in next hairpin lace loop of 2nd strip, * ch 2, sc in next loop of 1st strip, ch 2, sc in next hairpin lace loop of 2nd strip, repeat from * once, ** ch 2, sc in next loop of 1st strip, ch 2, sc through next 5 hairpin lace loops of 2nd strip, * ch 2, sc in next loop of 1st strip, ch 2, sc in next hairpin lace loop of 2nd strip, repeat from * 6 times, repeat from ** 9 times, ch 2, sc in next loop of 1st strip, ch 2, sc through next 5 hairpin lace loops of 2nd strip, * ch 2, sc in next loop of 1st strip, ch 2, sc in next hairpin lace loop of 2nd strip, repeat from * 3 times, cut thread. Working on opposite side of 2nd strip, attach Gold Spangle through 1st 3 loops, * ch 5, sc in next loop, repeat from * 6 times, ** ch 5, sc through next 5 loops, * ch 5, sc in next loop, repeat from * 6 times, repeat from ** 9 times, ch 5, sc through next 3 loops, cut thread.

3rd Strip: With Gold Spangle and 3 inch hairpin lace strip of 155 loops, attach thread in 1st hairpin lace loop, ch 2, sc in last loop worked of 2nd strip, ch 2, sc in next hairpin lace loop of 3rd strip, * ch 2, sc in next loop of 2nd strip, ch 2, sc in next hairpin lace loop of 3rd strip, repeat from * once, ** ch 2, sc in next loop of 2nd strip, ch 2, sc through next 7 hairpin lace loops of 3rd strip, * ch 2, sc in next loop of 2nd strip, ch 2, sc in next hairpin lace loop of 3rd strip, repeat from * 6 times, repeat from ** 9 times, ch 2, sc in next loop of 2nd strip, ch 2, sc through next 7 hairpin lace loops of 3rd strip, * ch 2, sc in next loop of 2nd strip, ch 2, sc in next hairpin lace loop of 3rd strip, repeat from * 3 times, cut thread. Working on opposite side of 3rd strip attach Gold Spangle through 1st 4 loops, * ch 7, sc in next loop, repeat from * 6 times, ** ch 7, sc through next 7 loops, * ch 7, sc in next loop, repeat from * 6 times, repeat from ** 9 times, ch 7, sc through next 4 loops, cut thread.

4th Strip: With Gold Spangle and 3 inch hairpin lace strip of 177 loops, attach thread in 1st hairpin lace loop, ch 3, sc in last loop worked of 3rd strip, ch 3, sc in next hairpin lace loop of 4th strip, * ch 3, sc in next loop of 3rd strip, ch 3, sc in next hairpin lace loop of 4th strip, repeat from * once, ** ch 3, sc in next loop of 3rd strip, ch 3, sc through next 9 hairpin lace loops of 4th strip, ch 3, sc in next loop of 3rd strip, ch 3, sc in next hairpin lace loop of 4th strip, repeat from * 6 times, repeat from ** 9 times, ch 3, sc in next loop of 3rd strip, ch 3, sc through next 9 hairpin lace loops of 4th strip, * ch 3, sc in next loop of 3rd strip, ch 3, sc in next hairpin lace loop of 4th strip, repeat from * 3 times, cut thread. Working on opposite side of 4th strip, attach Gold Spangle through 1st 5 loops, * ch 7, sc in next loop, repeat from * 6 times, ** ch 7, sc through next 9 loops, * ch 7, sc in next loop, repeat from * 6 times, repeat from ** 9 times, ch 7, sc through next 5 loops, cut thread.

5th Strip: With Gold Spangle and 4 inch hairpin lace strip of 199 loops, attach thread in 1st loop, ch 3, sc in last loop worked of 4th strip, ch 3, sc in next hairpin lace loop of 5th strip, * ch 3, sc in next loop of 4th strip, ch 3, sc in next hairpin lace loop of 5th strip. Repeat from * once, ** ch 3, sc in next loop of 4th strip, ch 3, sc through next 11 hairpin lace loops of 5th strip, * ch 3, sc in next loop of 4th strip, ch 3, sc in next hairpin lace loop of 5th strip, repeat from * 6 times, repeat from ** 9 times, ch 3, sc in next loop of 4th strip, ch 3, sc through next 11 hairpin lace loops of 5th strip, * ch 3, sc in next loop of 4th strip, ch 3, sc in next hairpin lace loop of 5th strip, repeat from * 3 times, cut thread. Working on opposite side of 5th strip, attach Gold Spangle through 1st 6 loops, * ch 9, sc in next loop, repeat from * 6 times, ** ch 9, sc through next 11 loops, * ch 9, sc in next loop, repeat from * 6 times, repeat from ** 9 times, ch 9, sc through next 6 loops, cut thread.

Neck Band: With wrong side of 1st row toward you attach Gold Spangle in 1st sc, sc in same space, then work 1 sc in each sc and in each ch 1 space, ch 1 to turn all rows.

Next Row: Working over entire st by inserting hook under entire st, work 1 sc in each sc.

Next 5 Rows: 1 sc in each sc.

Next Row: 1 slip stitch (sl st) in each sc, cut thread. Sew 2 hooks and eyes on wrong side of neck band.

Long Cape: Work 1st 5 strips same as short cape. With Gold Spangle and 4 inch hairpin lace strip of 221 loops, attach thread in 1st loop, ch 4, sc in last loop worked of 5th strip, ch 4, sc in next hairpin lace loop of 6th strip, * ch 4, sc in next loop of 5th strip, ch 4, sc in next hairpin lace loop of 6th strip, repeat from * once, ** ch 4, sc in next loop of 5th strip, ch 4, sc through next 13 hairpin lace loops of 6th strips, * ch 4, sc in next loop of 5th strip, ch 4, sc in next hairpin lace loop of 6th strip, repeat from * 6 times, repeat from ** 9 times, ch 4, sc in next loop of 5th strip, ch 4, sc through next 13 hairpin lace loops of 6th strip, * ch 4, sc in next loop of 5th strip, ch 4, sc in next hairpin lace loop of 6th strip, repeat from * 3 times, cut thread. Working on opposite side of 6th strip attach Gold Spangle through 1st 7 loops, * ch 9, sc in next loop, repeat from * 6 times, ** ch 9, sc through next 13 loops, * ch 9, sc in next loop, repeat from * 6 times, repeat from ** 9 times, ch 9, sc through next 7 loops, cut thread. Work neck band same as short cape.

Concerto

18 inches x 66 inches without fringe

Materials Required:

AMERICAN THREAD COMPANY

"DAWN" NYLON or NYLON POMPADOUR or
"DAWN" SWEATER & SOCK YARN
("SANFORLAN" WON'T SHRINK OUT OF FIT)
13 ounces Lt. Blue or Baby Blue or color of your choice
Plastic crochet hook size E

Gauge: 3 popcorn sts = 1 inch

Chain (ch) 113, double crochet (dc) in 8th stitch (st) from hook, * ch 2, skip 2 sts of ch, dc in next st, repeat from * across row (16 meshes), ch 4, turn.

2nd Row: Dc in next dc, ch 1, dc in same space, ch 1, dc in same space, ch 1, dc in next dc, * ch 1, 3 dc with ch 1 between each dc in next dc (shell), ch 1, dc in next dc, repeat from * once, ** ch 1, popcorn st in next dc (popcorn st: 6 dc in same space, drop loop from hook, insert hook in 1st dc, pick up loop and pull through), ch 2, popcorn st in next dc, ch 2, popcorn st in next dc, ch 1, dc in next dc, * ch 1, shell in next dc, ch 1, dc in next dc, repeat from * twice, repeat from ** 3 times, ending last repeat with ch 1, skip 1 st of end ch, dc in next st, ch 4, turn.

3rd Row: * Dc in center dc of next shell, ch 1, skip last dc of same shell, shell in next dc, ch 1, repeat from * twice, dc in next popcorn st, * ch 2, dc in next popcorn st, repeat from * once, ch 1, shell in next dc, ch 1, repeat from beginning 3 times, * dc in center dc of next shell, ch 1, skip last dc of same shell, shell in next dc, ch 1, repeat from * once, dc in center dc of next shell, ch 1, dc in 3rd st of end ch, ch 4, turn.

4th Row: Shell in next dc, ch 1, dc in center dc of next shell, * ch 1, skip last dc of same shell, shell in next dc, ch 1, dc in center dc of next shell, repeat from * once, ** ch 1, popcorn st in dc over the popcorn st of 2nd row below, * ch 2, popcorn st in next dc, repeat from * once, * ch 1, dc in center dc of next shell, ch 1, skip last dc of same shell, shell in next dc, repeat from * twice, ch 1, dc in center dc of next shell, repeat from ** 3 times ending last repeat with ch 1, dc in 3rd st of end ch, ch 1, turn.

Repeat the 3rd and 4th rows until stole measures 66 inches ending with 4th row of pattern.

Next Row: * Dc in center dc of next shell, ch 2, skip last dc of same shell, dc in next dc, ch 2, repeat from * twice, * dc in next popcorn st, ch 2, repeat from * twice, dc in next dc, ch 2, repeat from beginning 3 times, * dc in center dc of next shell, ch 2, skip last dc of same shell, dc in next dc, ch 2, repeat from * once, dc in center dc of next shell, ch 2, dc in 3rd st of end ch (46 meshes), cut yarn.

Fringe: Wind yarn over an 18 inch cardboard, cut one end. Using 8 strands, double in half and knot through every other mesh of last row.

Next Row: * Take half of one group of fringe and half of next group of fringe, knot together ½ inch from 1st row of knots, repeat from * across row.

Next Row: Take each group of fringe and knot about ½ inch from last row of knots.

Next Row: * Take half of one group of fringe and half of next group of fringe, knot together ½ inch from last row of knots, repeat from * across row. Trim fringe evenly. Finish opposite end to correspond.

Minuet

Materials Required:

AMERICAN THREAD COMPANY

"DAWN" SWEATER & SOCK YARN ("SANFORLAN"—WON'T SHRINK OUT OF FIT) or "DAWN" NYLON or NYLON POMPADOUR
7-ounces Med. Pink or Lt. Pink or color of your choice.
1 pair knitting needles No. 7
3 hooks and eyes, 2 yds. 3 inch satin ribbon.
Steel crochet hook No. 1

Gauge: 11 sts = 2 inches7 rows = 1 inch

Starting at neck edge cast on 181 stitches (sts) and work 7 rows in stockinette st [Knit (K) 1 row, Purl (P) 1 row].

8th Row: K across row on Purl side to form a ridge.

Next 8 Rows: Work in stockinette st starting with a K row.

17th Row: K 36, * increase 1 st in next st, K 17, repeat from * 5 times, increase 1 st in next st, K 36.

Next 7 Rows: Work even in stockinette st starting with a P row.

25th Row: K across row, increasing 7 sts and keeping increases in line with previous increases.

Repeat last 8 rows twice.

Next 4 Rows: Work even in stockinette st.

Repeat from 8th row 3 more times, having 7 increases in each increasing row keeping increases in line with previous increases.

Repeat from 8th through 29th row once.

Next Row: K across row on Purl side.

Next 7 Rows: Work even in stockinette st. Bind off loosely.

Finishing: Fold along first ridge at neck edge, turn under the first 7 rows and sew to form hem. Fold along last ridge and hem. Now fold along each of the 4 center ridges to form 1¼ inch tucks and sew in place. At right front edge sew 1st tuck ½ inch below top ridge, sew 2nd tuck ½ inch below ridge of 1st tuck. Pin next 2 ridges together and sew to top corner. Finish left front edge in

same manner. Tack tucks in position 5 inches in from front edge. Work a row of single crochet (sc) along front edges. Sew hooks and eyes in position. Finish with bow as illustrated.

Fantasy

18 inches x 60 inches without fringe

Materials Required:

AMERICAN THREAD COMPANY

"DAWN" ORLON or ORLON POMPADOUR
High Bulk Fingering Yarn
7 ounces White or color of your choice
Plastic crochet hook size G or H

Chain (ch) 256 (to measure about 61 inches), double crochet (dc) in 6th stitch (st) from hook, * ch 1, skip 1 st of ch, dc in next st of ch, repeat from * to end of ch (126 meshes), ch 2, turn.

2nd Row: Draw up a loop in 2nd st from hook, in 1st dc in next ch 1 space and in next dc (5 loops on hook), yarn over and draw through all loops at one time, ch 1, * draw up a loop through the ch 1 just made (the ch 1 is termed the eye of star st), draw up a loop in same st already worked in, in next ch 1 space and in next dc (5 loops on hook), yarn over and draw through all loops at one time, ch 1, repeat from * across row ending last star st by drawing a loop through 3rd st of end ch, ch 4, turn.

3rd Row: Dc in eye of next star st, * ch 1, dc in eye of next star st, repeat from * across row ending row with ch 1, dc in turning ch, ch 2, turn.

Repeat 2nd and 3rd rows until work measures 18 inches ending with a mesh row, cut yarn.

Fringe: Wind yarn over a 3 inch cardboard, cut one end. Using 4 strands double in half and loop through each row on each short end.

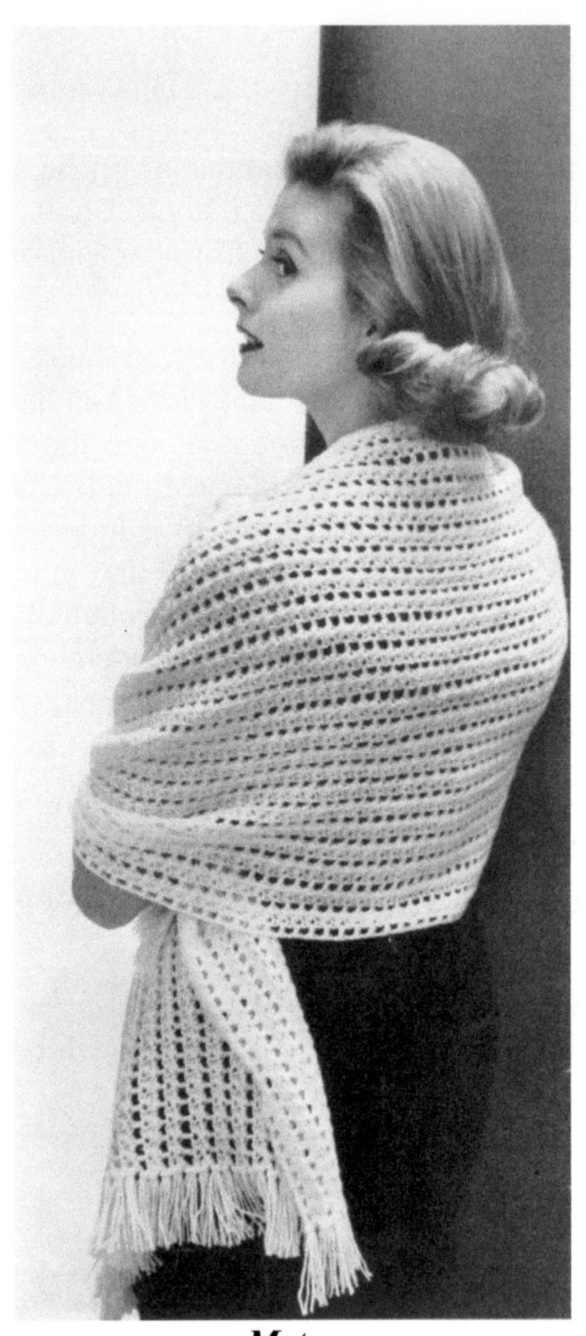

Metron

32 inches x 32 inches without fringe

Materials Required:

AMERICAN THREAD COMPANY

"DAWN" SWEATER & SOCK YARN (SANFORLAN—"WON'T SHRINK OUT OF FIT") or "DAWN" NYLON or NYLON POMPADOUR

8 ounces White or color of your choice

1 pr. knitting needles No. 9

Gauge: 5 garter sts = 1 inch

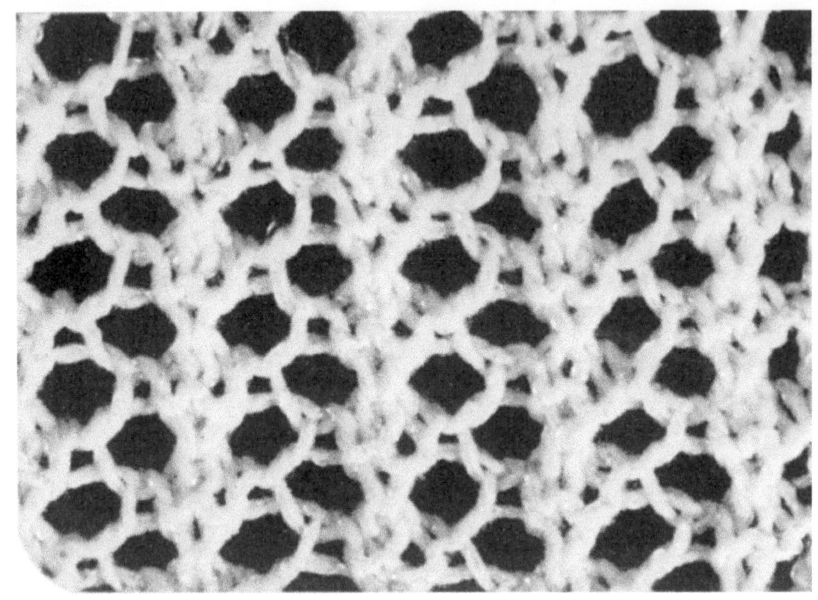

Cast on 137 stitches (sts) loosely and Knit (K) 1 row.

2nd Row: K 4, * yarn over (y o), slip (sl) 1, K 2 together (tog), pass slip stitch over K stitch (p.s.s.o.), y o, K 3, repeat from * across row ending last repeat with K 4.

3rd Row: K across row.

4th Row: K 1, * y o, sl 1, K 2 tog, p.s.s.o., y o, K 3, repeat from * across row ending last repeat with K 1.

5th Row: K across row.

Repeat the last 4 rows 10 times.

Next Row: K 4, * y o, sl 1, K 2 tog, p.s.s.o., y o, K 3, repeat from * twice, y o, sl 1, K 2 tog, p.s.s.o., y o, K 87,

* y o, sl 1, K 2 tog, p.s.s.o., y o, K 3, repeat from * twice, y o, sl 1, K 2 tog, p.s.s.o., y o, K 4.

Next Row: K across row.

Next Row: K 1, * y o, sl 1, K 2 tog, p.s.s.o., y o, K 3, repeat from * twice, y o, sl 1, K 2 tog, p.s.s.o., y o, K 93, * y o, sl 1, K 2 tog, p.s.s.o., y o, K 3, repeat from * twice, y o, sl 1, K 2 tog, p.s.s.o., y o, K 1.

Next Row: K across row. Repeat the last 4 rows 47 times. Repeat 2nd, 3rd, 4th and 5th rows 10 times, then repeat 2nd, 3rd and 4th rows once, bind off.

Fringe: Wind yarn over an 8½ inch cardboard, cut one end. Using 4 strands, double in half and knot through each hole across starting end and finishing end. Cut strands same length for each side but place 1st fringe in 1st hole, * skip next hole, place a fringe in next garter st row, skip next hole, place a fringe in next hole, repeat from * across side. Finish opposite side in same manner. * Using half of 1 group of fringe and half of next group of fringe knot together about ½ inch from last row of knots, repeat from * all around.

Lyric

19 inches x 64 inches without fringe

Materials Required:

AMERICAN THREAD COMPANY

"DAWN" BABY YARN or
"DAWN" MEDIUM WEIGHT
POMPADOUR
12 ounces Baby Pink or color of your choice
Steel crochet hook No. 0

Gauge: Each strip measures 2½ inches in width

1st Strip—1st Half: Chain (ch) 10, join to form a ring, ch 3, work 17 double crochet (dc) in ring, join, turn.

2nd Row: Ch 4, dc in next dc, * ch 1, dc in next dc, repeat from * 7 times, ch 5, dc in same space, ch 1, turn.

3rd Row: 1 single crochet (sc), ch 5, 4 sc in large loop, * 1 sc, ch 4, 1 sc in next ch 1 space, 2 sc in next ch 1 space, repeat from * once, 1 sc, ch 4, 1 sc in next ch 1 space, 1 sc in next ch 1 space, ch 7, turn, skip 2 sc, the ch 4 and 2 sc, slip stitch (sl st) in next sc, ch 3, turn, work 8 dc over loop, ch 3, sl st in same loop, sc in next ch 1 space already worked in 1 sc, ch 4, 1 sc in next ch 1 space, 2 sc next ch 1 space, ch 5, turn.

4th Row: Skip 3 sc, ch 4 and 2 sc, dc in next ch 3 loop, * ch 1 dc in next st, repeat from * 8 times, ch 5, skip 1 sc, ch 4 and 2 sc, sl st in next sc, ch 1, turn.

Repeat the 3rd and 4th rows until there are 32 scallops.

Next Row: 4 sc, ch 5, 4 sc in large loop, * 1 sc, ch 4, 1 sc in next ch 1 space, 2 sc in next ch 1 space, repeat from * 3 times, 1 sc, ch 4, 1 sc in next loop, working along side of strip, * 4 sc, ch 5, 4 sc in next large loop, 1 sc, ch 4, 1 sc in next loop, repeat from * to center, cut yarn.

1st Strip—2nd Half: With wrong side of work toward you, attach yarn in last dc of last loop of 2nd row of 1st half, * ch 1, dc in next st, repeat from * 8 times, ch 5, join in 3rd st of ch at beginning of 2nd row, ch 1, turn.

3rd and 4th Rows: Same as 3rd and 4th rows of 1st half of strip. Repeat the 3rd and 4th rows until there are 32 scallops.

Next Row: Same as last row of 1st half of strip.

2nd Strip—1st Half: Work same as 1st half of 1st Strip joining in last row as follows: 4 sc, ch 5, 4 sc in large loop, * 1 sc, ch 4, 1 sc in next ch 1 space, 2 sc in next ch 1 space, repeat from * 3 times, 1 sc, ch 4, 1 sc in next loop, 4 sc in next loop, ch 2, join to corresponding loop of 1st half of 1st strip (1st ch 5 loop at side end of strip), working along sides of both strips, ch 2, 4 sc in same loop of 2nd strip, 1 sc, ch 4, 1 sc in next loop, * 4 sc in next loop, ch 2, skip next ch 4 loop, join to next ch 5 loop of 1st strip, ch 2, 4 sc in same loop of 2nd strip, 1 sc, ch 4, 1 sc in next loop, repeat from * 29 times, cut yarn.

2nd Strip—2nd Half: With wrong side of work toward you attach yarn in last dc of 2nd row of 1st half, * ch 1, dc next st, repeat from * 8 times, ch 5, join in 3rd st of ch at beginning of 2nd row, ch 1, turn.

3rd Row: 4 sc in large loop, ch 2, join to corresponding loop of opposite strip, ch 2, 4 sc in same loop, * 1 sc, ch 4, 1 sc in next ch 1 space, 2 sc in next ch 1 space, repeat from * once, 1 sc, ch 4, 1 sc in next ch 1 space, 1 sc in next ch 1 space, ch 7, turn, skip 2 sc, the ch 4 and 2 sc, sl st in next sc, ch 3, turn, work 8 dc over loop, ch 3, sl st in same loop, sc in next ch 1 space already worked in, 1 sc, ch 4, 1 sc in next ch 1 space, 2 sc in next ch 1 space, ch 5, turn.

4th Row: Skip 2 sc, ch 4 and 2 sc, dc in next ch 3 loop, * ch 1, dc in next st, repeat from * 8 times, ch 5, skip 1 sc, ch 4 and 2 sc, sl st in next sc, ch 1, turn.

Repeat the 3rd and 4th rows until there are 32 scallops.

Next Row: Work same as last row of 2nd half of 1st strip. Work 6 more strips in same manner.

Fringe: Wind yarn over an 8½ inch cardboard. Cut one end. Using 6 strands, double in half and knot through each of the 5 picots at lower edge of each strip.

9 798330 240272

Printed by Libri Plureos GmbH in Hamburg,
Germany